ERGO

ALSO BY MICHELENE WANDOR

ERGO
NEW POEMS
Michelene Wandor

2024

Published by Arc Publications
Nanholme Mill, Shaw Wood Road
Todmorden OL14 6DA, UK
www.arcpublications.co.uk

978 1911469 75 9

Design by Tony Ward
Printed in Great Britain by
TJ Books, Padstow, Cornwall

Cover photograph © Adam Victor
by kind permission of the photographer

Arc Chapbook Series
Series Editor: Tony Ward

CONTENTS

PART ONE

FIELD

yellows show through frost, streaking wet
with melting
winter has toughened, frail leaves flung, sneer-blown
to be kicked

heavy gloves worry the machines, frozen before
anti-freeze could anti-freeze
spark plugs spark, and
winter is simple for some

at night my words come into a circle of light
syllables into arbitrary meaning, themselves silent
somewhere someone learns through ignorance

AMERICAN CEMETERY

Harley-Davison roars splat, spattering
fumes, toxic, noxious, an
American dream, dreaming

face, lips tongued, arrogance twanged
through narrow lanes, across
flat fields, nose to gate, a gale gently starting
an East Anglian farmer bends, shielding his eyes from
the wind's tears, no time to bid the day across

rows of white crosses growing from the ground sweep
by the bike's side   American mothers dream
of their sons, no longer dreaming, no longer able
to dream by themselves

my legs streak splashed mud from careless wheels
a leather back streaks away

I am alone, doing nothing
and nothing crosses my mind, not even a dream

of the crazy phase of love, leaving
streaks of dried mud on – let's face it – my heart

LOVE AGAIN

I have a clairvoyant past, though
the present never measures up to it
even when I look up from a book
to rehearse the world's
shape

weather whispers behind night-time
melting dirt on the tracks, more snow
themes

brown from much travel, firm, oiled with
digested information made into more news
nothing jaded about his hands, finely
flying over mine
                'one is what one is'
trips easily from him, not
bothering to know what one is or
might be

SPRING

snowdrop flakes on my doorstep
bores down through concrete
out of its depth

I sympathise, my foot frozen in the March snow
put the flower in an egg-cup, where
not surprisingly, it dies

beware of sympathy
beware of surprise

CARE

orange Christmas, a tree, tiny with shiny
promise
stunt stalk, stuck straight, thick
sure leaves

I water it, watching
the wet in passing

but the leaves tire
the stalk wanes, pines
                    one of us
has not tried hard enough

STICK MAN

protesting against unnecessary war, we wear
black arm bands
                    even without lunch, my
children are well, relatively
they drew me a picture of a
stick man, and I pitied it

FOSSIL

locked stones on the sand, bar all comers
rock-year billions, unyielding, except for the daring
dragonfly unwary

he broke his heart-wing against a jagged edge
eventually, he hopes the loving stone will admit him, if only
to impress
no chlorophyll, just honey holes and wings open for ever

STONED

the goldfish pond turned into a three-wheeler
bike and I pedalled into the sea

sandwiches in a colander, tortoise-shell
candy and gilded guavas

all our friends jumped on with swordfish rakes
and cut the sea down to size

ELY

houses almost
                    cower beside the towering cathedral
maintain a respectful distance
grass and low walls drizzle invisible dampness
we are a vacuum of lovers, having a
postcard day: the Grand Canyon chasing Damon
Runyon

we chew market apples

stone upon crossed stone, carved to
the bishop's breast, prone as he lies, tiny, chipped, almost
headless

the verger complains that some people
think the cathedral is there for their convenience
and not God's

GEOGRAPHY

desert   dust turned golden, fires
                  glow grey
                  no more wind, the dust not
stinging   the sun has pushed the night out

walking here, pitting strength, leaning forward, hands
dangled, loose and easy

the fire shimmers the waterhole rusty, maps held
firm, pointed fingers moving fast

once camels would have circled
not knowing that in our world, the night is
new and the year is new and geography stays
first footed

'the difference between us' anchors two
places between which we used to travel
sand is not sea, navigation is the difference
between us

the moment has gone and 'I'
was not included in the inverted commas

SEPARATION

separation and reparation furbish us
with all we need, lacquered tables and Scandinavian china
curtains of fine muslin, dotted with tiny gold flowers blow
ing in the wind

we sit in the middle of the floor, our horoscopes held in
a crystal Christmas snow paperweight, only
displaced when we turn up
side down

we melt into our own negatives, and events pass
through us

REPARATION

a swallow, pink against the hot summer sky
                    how we stare up
                                        it
turns black, a speck, far in the blue sky
I grope for your hand, not
looking down or around
                    for an instant I
hold a mistaken warm bird, soft

and then it flies, now a white pigeon in a dull grey sky
imagining Big Ben's fine Cadbury flake pinnacles, where
they melt decisions of state

and send messages to the people, that's
you and me

FOREST FIRE

haze has
      fired underground dry resin, unprompted clouds
   rise
pining red through the wind changing yesterday's
   green

the fire speaks sparks, cannot control its speech, a
person with too much to say and no order
in which to say it

the damage is measured in area and value by men who
received postcards from relatives last summer

their elbows are comfortable, though
some will have no tables this winter

VULTURE

vultures in the distance are dark
butterflies
         a moment of delicacy, wheeling into
a flower, a winding road above our heads

far distant, the feet still claw in silent clarity

just as we are used to the rhythm, the head modulates
and sweeps the horizon, marked only by
a dropped feather

BIRTHDAY

black night holds light inside, candles round
the birthday table, laughter round melons
with salt to bring out the sugar

on some heads, another hair will turn grey

LANDSCAPE

bees chasten the hillside   lavender
and rosemary fly higher, in search of jasmine
                              acacia

low brush-bushes dry bouquets of wild flowers
perfumes taste of honey and the brilliance of many scents

each tree pronounces a different shape   green
needles grip their own power

you sweep willows with your eyelashes, brush
the silver birch with your cheek and
circle the oak, joining hands and branches

this was called love, once, seasonal

BEACHED ROCKS

seahorse shapes with blurred distance, lavender
over the edge

heat haze expects a lady on her white charger to ride out
of her book, covering elegant distances
before coming into focus
a rubid sun, dim in-night
corrugated shimmers while she meets her love in the dark
a romantic love, this, too full of dreams

BETRAYAL

leeches drop like false entries in an index, someone
once told me, hiding their threats

I see a chink in your words, the size and
platitude of a magnifying glass

I would like to catch a scorpion and send
it off with a sting in its tail, but
the air is sucked out and your face is a vacuum, with
only a smile stuck on
leeching something

past the window of possibility
as if
a lie has gone unnoticed

THE NEW

you groan, past the stage of peeling ideas,
now you must swallow them whole, or not
at all
        I try putting it another way:
a sailboat in the harbour, two sails, one
white (large), one small (blue)
                          people with their
hands in their pockets, whistling, waiting
to crew
        when the tide is right

or another way: barrows tilted with fruit, wrapped
in their neat straw and purple paper nests

one day, I say, the trees will grow fruit like that, will lay their
fruit like battery chickens
                have you ever thought of that?

borrow my imagination for the day, I plead

INTIMACY

someone is committing intimacy, according to
an ancient text, barely decipherable

so gestures are sometimes bound to go astray
intimating

I taste your agony, sweetened with two lumps of
distance between us
in time

I couldn't know that disappointment would,
despite Chomsky and de
Saussure, have a very specific mean
ing

POETRY

once we had separated, the poems improved
night became a present for any day of the year

NIGHT

a hand, inside my window, replaces cup on wood,
china
grains mingle, stains spread in and out

I switch off the lamp
the moon still laughs
turns to moss, reminders of velvet fingers

night always brings that

NEGOTIATION

I see an uncharacteristic innocence in you

being uncharacteristic, I am disconcerted, and that is
uncharacteristic of me

perhaps there is
something we can discuss here?

LOSS

the year is bereft of its anchor
the quay stretches, soft with hot tarmac
marked with too many shocks
the ships still sail, their riggings
grabbed, reassuring, even
when becalmed

they have forgotten how to come to shore

PART TWO

ERGO

a snake sheds its skin into a poem
dry and feathery, swirling on a path
knowing not what knots it once knew

I hide inside doubt
I know what I know and
I seek I know not what in what I know

three bricks on a windowsill etch
my attention, a book
between each, leafed lightly like
an English moment when the sun has lifted

think of a subject
no shadow of silk or muslin folds, just
the clarity of calico paper

deduce a pronoun from the tone of voice

I talk you out into
the air, once warm, now cooling faster
than the speed of electricity
writing is as loud, but slower
I can't answer myself back

PLACE

the power of a place lies in its
claim on the past   a claim
made yesterday

imagine a postcard pinned to glass with
scratchy tenuousness, a window frame in
a house of cards

imagine a floor, straw-littered, boarded to
protect the new residents' heads from our
fragments

the walls are bare where
the bookcase used to stand
the plumbing revealed skeletal below the sink

glass cracked in the windows, the crack holds the
postcard, pinned   drawing
attention to straw dust on the floor

not easy to peer out, no more vista
nothing left but the power of the place, which
has little to do with any thing
and much to do with us

SONG

scroll down the side of your face as you leave
remember the eyes' intrigue, the accidental promise
of a hand's brush
the shape of lips curved into a smile

leap in, soft, caressing, taste
the warmth of words, the ebb
and swell of an unmeasurable caesura, with
no time for now

in this moment of departure
someone
has taken all your notes

TRAVEL

　　losing count after ten
spiral hairpins laid end to bend
climbing up, craning necks back
daring each corner to tip us

hills with dark green
luminous lights　　　　　　　from this
distance you push your hand against
the slope　　　　it springs down
against the pressure, moss-covered
bracken
　　　　　　　　perching on a rock high
above the road; dry garlic sausage, black
bread, fat dripping salt cucumbers; high
in the fir trees something slumps fat and
black as a bear
　　　　　we pack the empty bottle carefully

later, a monopoly of red roofs in a valley
bracketed unevenly between the mountain's sides
obscure day-to-day
farm gardens and yards
where land
and industry's smoke experiment
co-operation, where the mountain's view
of itself
sometimes catches its breath in
sheer impression

ISLAND

lace belies stone
face to the wall, no dust
on the dun-coloured linen

old ladies still weave
filigree dreams off
Fungus Rock, the inland sea
tickles the arid heights

a family squints into the shallow
salt pools, brushes white
crystals into heaps resting
against molten rock
prismatic in the sun

lava is a memory
stone roots burned into the ground

the mainland has been
adopted by machines; here
are still traces of
lace on stone

WILLOW PATTERN

tablecloth: best Irish linen, orange-dyed

tinkle over the edge   a porcelain dish
fell   damn it late

blue and white lovers
chasing across the bridge
'hurry up,
                they'll catch us'

you stand   look beyond
what you can see

imagine being the only people on a plate

you cannot cross the bridge
I wait

BIOGRAPHICAL NOTE

MICHELENE WANDOR is a playwright, poet, fiction writer, musician and cultural commentator. She was the first woman playwright to have a drama on one of the National Theatre's main stages – *The Wandering Jew* - in 1987, the same year her adaptation of *The Belle of Amherst* won an International Emmy for Thames TV. Her prolific radio drama includes original radio plays and dramatisations (novels by Dostoyevsky, Jane Austen, H. G. Wells, George Eliot, Kipling, Sara Paretsky and Margaret Drabble), many nominated for awards. Original plays include *Courtly Love*, about Isabella d'Este and Lucrezia Borgia, and *Tulips in Winter*, about the philosopher, Spinoza (both Radio 3). Her first novel, *Orfeo's Last Act*, about Monteverdi and the Jewish composer, Salamone Rossi, was published in 2023 by Greenwich Exchange.

She has taught Creative Writing for over four decades and was a Royal Literary Fund Fellow, 2004-2009. Her last four poetry collections are published by Arc Publications, with *Musica Transalpina* a Poetry Book Society Recommendation for 2006. *The Music of the Prophets*, a narrative poem about the resettlement of the Jews in England, was supported by an award from the European Association for Jewish Culture. Her work has been praised by Elaine Feinstein, Peter Porter and Peter Riley.